POEMS OF A SON

PRAYERS OF A FATHER

Judson Press® Valley Forge

POEMS OF
A SON

PRAYERS
OF
A FATHER

Matthew L. Watley
William D. Watley

To Matthew A. Watley

Father and Grandfather

Library of Congress Cataloging-in-Publication Data

Watley, Matthew L.
    Poems of a son, prayers of a father/Matthew L. Watley, William D. Watley.
        p.   cm.
    Summary: The poems of a teenage Afro-American boy about his thoughts and feelings are accompanied by prayers his father wrote in response to the poems.
    ISBN 0-8170-1183-8
    1. Afro-American teenagers—Poetry. 2. Afro-Americans—Poetry. 3. Prayers. [1. American poetry. 2. Afro-Americans—Poetry. 3. Prayers.]
I. Watley, William D. II. Title
PS3573.A846P64   1992
811'.54—dc20   92-11599
                                                   CIP

Printed in the U.S.A.
05 04 03 02 01 00 99 98 97 96
11 10 9 8 7 6 5 4 3 2

Contents

Foreword 9

Preface 11

POEMS and PRAYERS

    Grandfather 14

    The Road 16

    The Sculptor 18

    Dear God... 20

    To Fall in Love 22

    Dreams 24

    Peepholes 26

    Sunset 28

    Pressure 30

    The Night 32

    Glory 34

    Mighty Pollution 38

    I Grow Weary 40

    One of Those Days 42

    Thanks for the rain 44

    Faith 46

    Evolution 48

    The Past, the Present, or the Future? 50

    It Is Too Late 52

    Two Men 54

    She 56

    The Drug Wars 58

    Run Away 60

    Just a Dance 62

    Behold Thy Mother 64

    The Field 66

    Jennifer, My Sister 68

    Rage 70

    My Never Love 72

    My Utopian Existence 74

    Domination 76

    Taking a Stand 80

    Different Paths 82

    Death 84

    After 86

    The Legacy Continues—A Son's Prayer 88

Foreword

It is truly a blessing to have loved and been loved by a father, to honor his values, be inspired by his dreams, and want to make him proud of you. It is also a blessing to love and be loved by a son, to respect his values, have faith in his dreams, and be filled with pride at his accomplishments. This love is not just a legacy that is passed from generation to generation, like a baton in a relay race. It is shared, unconditional, an endless rope by which each generation is pulled up toward the mountaintop, elevating all beyond the mortality of their lifetimes. This shared love (what the Rev. Matthew A. Watley, to whom this book is dedicated, might have known as *agape* love), drives and uplifts *Poems of a Son, Prayers of a Father.*

It is only natural that I find this book personally inspiring, insightful, and uplifting. I am one of many African American men blessed by a father whom I admired and respected and a son—actually, three sons—to whom I have entrusted the future. From my father and namesake, Earl G. Graves, a hard-working second-generation Barbadian, I learned the rewards of self-discipline, productive labor, and commitment to family. I also benefited from his passion for things beyond his reach during his lifetime, including his dream of business ownership. While my father died before fulfilling his entrepreneurial ambitions, his oldest son is now the CEO of two of the nation's largest black-owned enterprises. I am also sharing that dream with my sons, two of whom work as executives in my businesses and the third, a successful attorney. Earl Jr., John, and Michael have been strengthened as much by the legacy of their grandfather as they have been shaped by the love of their father. He taught me the value of reaching beyond one's grasp, and I have passed that lesson on to my sons.

The prayers and prose of the book you are now holding pay tribute to the shared dreams of African American men. But anyone, regardless of race or gender, who loves a father, son, husband, brother, or uncle will find this book a priceless treasure. The gospel tells us that God so loved the world that he gave his only begotten son. William and Matthew Watley's collaboration shows just how wondrously powerful even an infinitesimal portion of such love can be.

Earl G. Graves
Editor and Publisher, BLACK ENTERPRISE
CEO, Pepsi-Cola of Washington, D.C., Ltd.

Preface

In the midst of all the writings about the African American male as an endangered species and all the discussions about the number of African American households headed by females, the impression is sometimes unwittingly given that the African American male is a nonentity in black life and culture. It is implied that even when he is present in the home, he assumes the role of the "invisible man." This, however, is not the case. There is such a creature as the strong and responsible married African American male who is a hard-working and loving companion to his spouse and is a protective and positive influence in the life of his children.

Many of us in the African American community know this to be true. My father, the Reverend Matthew A. Watley, was a prototype of manhood who was ethnically conscious without being racist, strict without being overbearing, principled without being unbending, humorous without being silly, tough without being hardened, and prayerful in all things. He was a man of faith and pride who by precept and example taught me how to be a husband and father. I have tried to pass on the same legacy to my son, Matthew.

Our family history is being repeated in innumerable African American families. This book is but one example of the ways that African American manhood interfaces and exchanges its gifts and values from one generation to another.

This collaborative writing project has been an exciting one for Matthew and me. I discovered his poetic gift several years ago when his mother showed me a group of poems he had written for a school project. Since I am not a poet, I have always been in awe of persons who are able to express themselves in verse form—particularly when it rhymes. I was impressed not only with his poetry, but also with the depth of feeling and the breadth of thought that are represented.

Matthew and I both share a foundation of faith that causes us to think deeply about a number of issues. God's Creative Spirit, as reflected in Matthew's faith pilgrimage, moves Matthew to write poetry. The Holy Spirit moves me to sermonize and pray. Thus, *Poems of a Son, Prayers of a Father* chronicles an intergenerational dialogue sparked by a common faith and the shared experience of being African American and male in today's world. Each of Matthew's poems is followed by a prayer I have written in response to the feelings and thoughts expressed in the poem.

We bow in sacred memory to Matthew's grandfather and my father, the late Matthew A. Watley. I have dedicated other works to him. However,

11

it seemed appropriate and fitting to dedicate this first joint venture between his son, whom he referred to as "my favorite preacher," and his grandson, whom he called "Grandpa's boy," to him. We also remember all of the other men of African American descent among our family relations and in our friendship circle who have helped shape us into the men that we are. Especially do we remember the late Noah Batson, as well as William Day and Lawrence Lewis.

In addition, we thank the women in our family whose image and imprint we also bear—Muriel Watley, wife and mother, Jennifer Elaine, daughter and sister, as well as Marian Watley, Noretta Vaught, Palecia Lewis, and Smythe Batson.

For assistance in the technical preparation of this manuscript as well as for their invaluable input, we are grateful to Carolyn Scavella—sister, friend, and Aunt Cee-Cee—and Constance Wright, administrative assistant and big sister. We are grateful indeed to Judson Press for their willingness to publish this unique work.

Peace,
William D. Watley
Matthew L. Watley
Fall 1991

Grandfather

With his hope, with his heart, and sometimes with his hands
He molded me into the man that I am.
With his life, with his love, and his rousing laughter
He left me a legacy to pattern myself after.

Full of wisdom and knowledge, but not distant or apart
He was more than a teacher, for he lived what he taught.
Noble and strong, he was the embodiment of all
That I've desired to be since I was small.

My veins pulse with his blood,
My heart soars with his love;
My feet follow the path to God,
The same path that he first trod.

Then our bond became strained by his health
As he became weaker with haste and stealth.
Yet we grasped each other stronger
To make our time together longer.

Then finally it broke
And I was parted from his yoke,
Leaving me alone to stand
In memory of this mighty black man.

O God, thank you for my father. Thank you for his love that cared enough to discipline me. Sometimes I was afraid of him because he seemed so big when I was such a small boy. I am truly grateful that he was with me long enough for me to understand that sometimes tender love must be expressed in tough ways so that the young and tender life it cares about and is trying to mold will be better prepared to handle life and all of its toughness.

Thank you, God, for my father, for his selfless labor of love on behalf of those he cared about—the church of his membership, the churches he pastored, and his family. I praise you for his example that showed the real meaning of being a shepherd of God's people. I praise you for his cutting criticism in my early preaching days and for his insistence on solid and thorough preparation before your word is proclaimed to your people.

O God, my ministry has been blessed in many, many ways. Sometimes I wonder if some of my blessings are because of his sacrifices. Thank you for blessing me through him and for allowing this son to bring some joy to his father.

O God, I do not understand why he had to leave us when he did. You know how much I miss him. When the weight of pastoring bears down upon my shoulders, when I am discouraged, frustrated, lonely, angry, and confused, you know how much I miss not being able to pick up a phone and talk with him.

Yet, God, in spite of all that I don't understand, I trust you and I love you. I know that you're too wise to make mistakes and that you do not burden the hearts of your children unnecessarily. For everything you do there is a reason.

So I do not begrudge Daddy his rest, and I am grateful that you are patient with my doubts and questions and that you are always there for me to talk with. In his absence, God, I've learned to talk to you more.

Thank you, God, for Daddy. Thank you that he lived long enough for my son to know him and call his name blessed. Now, God, help me to be to my son all that my father was to both of us. I can't do it without you, God; I don't have to try, for you are always with me—Father to the fatherless, Mother to the motherless.

Thank you, God, for my daddy, my son, and for just being you. Amen.

The Road

As I begin to grow in mind and soul,
I find myself unfit for life's unrest.
Without the means to catch and hold my goal,
I feel the pain that comes with this stress.

The ladder that I climb is very old;
With every rung I feel it quake.
It bends and shakes as if it would fold;
I cower feeling that my life's at stake.

The road of my life has many turns
That hamper my sight of what's in store.
The fear of the unknown within me burns;
I know it must be doused with life's rich lore.

Encouraged by the training of my years
I start upon the road despite my fears.

Mother and Father God, the road that leads from dreams to goals, from birth to eternity with you, can be a long and frightening one. However, we praise you right now because we don't have to walk that road alone. You have been with us and you have promised to be with us every step of the way. We must confess, Lord, that sometimes we feel lonely as we walk down life's uneven, meandering, and ofttimes bumpy road. In those moments of desolation we pray for discernment as you come close in special ways even as you did to the two disciples on the Emmaus road on the first Easter evening many years ago. When we become headstrong and wrong, we pray that your loving hand would halt us and that we would receive a new revelation of you and a new word about the purpose of our lives—even as you came to Saul on the Damascus road.

And if trouble overtakes us along the way, as it did the man on the Jericho road, we pray for faith that informs our spirit that your eyes are still upon us and that by-and-by, help and deliverance will come. When we tread Gaza's desert road, we pray that the promise of your Word will come alive for us as it did for an Ethiopian eunuch long ago.

We can start down the road despite our fears because we know that you are with us. We bow before you with the faith of John Greenleaf Whittier who penned the words:

> I know not where His islands lift
> Their fronded palms in air;
> I only know I cannot drift
> Beyond His love and care.[1]

Thank you, God, for our journey. Amen.

---

[1] From "The Eternal Goodness."

The Sculptor

Honed from a stone unflawed, pure and whole,
Not quartered and sectioned like a piece of coal,
But smooth and dense, heavy and hard,
It's surface seemingly protected from being scarred.

A figure is born first from a drizzle
Turning into a downpour of strikes and hits
Upon the stone by a mallet and chisel.
The defenseless rock gravely sits

As the sculptor chips away at it's sides,
Not to create, but rather to reveal
The figure that inside the rock hides,
Setting free from the rock what has been instilled.

O Sculptor of life, busy your hands;
I stand before you a half-finished man.
Use your tools of experience, your tools of life,
Your mallet and chisel of happiness and strife
To chip at the rock until I am perfected
And you in me are fully reflected.

O Creator God, you who knows us better than we know ourselves, we come before you as willing and pliable instruments of divine providence, ready to be used by you for noble and great purposes. You know our strengths and weaknesses, our potential and capabilities, and so we trust your judgment.

Help us to affirm the gifts and graces that you have placed within each of us. We must confess, God, that sometimes we think of ourselves more highly than we ought and resist and rebel against your leadership because we are pursuing projects and timetables that our egos tell us we can handle. We confess that sometimes we think we ought to have a larger and more glorious role than the place you have assigned to us. We must confess, Lord, that sometimes we become caricatures and vulgar imitations of others because we have not accepted the self that you have made and are molding. Forgive us for walking upon our own determined and sometimes self-centered paths that lead to mediocrity rather than the prize of the high calling.

O God, we are so grateful that you think enough of us to use us in your service. O God, we pray that our lives will glorify you. Forgive us when we complain and doubt your word and fail to remember your unbroken promises as we walk by faith in fields of service. Forgive us for our shortsightedness, our proclivity toward yielding to our weaknesses rather than having eyes that are focused solely on the glory of God. We know that you who have begun a good work in us are able to bring it to completion at the day of Jesus Christ. So, Divine Sculptor, you who know what's best for us, have your own way with us. We love you so much and trust you so much that each of us can pray

> Have Thine own way, Lord! Have Thine own way!
> Thou art the Potter, I am the clay.
> Mold me and make me after Thy will,
> While I am waiting yielded and still.[2]

Amen.

---

[2]From "Have Thine Own Way, Lord," by Adelaide A. Pollard.

Dear God...

Dear God, if you please, let me be paranoid.
I know this sounds like the strangest request,
But it's the only thing that can fill this void,
And until it is filled, I'll find no rest.

It seems today that the world is against me,
The only reason being that my skin is black.
I try to convince myself this just isn't true,
Yet all of the evidence shows it as fact.

I see poor education and unequal chances.
I see people mistreated—their skin like mine.
I am told these things don't really exist,
But I just don't think they're all in my mind.

Why then would I still not believe?
Because I'd lose all my hope, I'd lose all faith.
If I accepted my suspicions simply as truth,
Then wouldn't this world be an evil place?

So God, you must see the need for me to be paranoid,
Then this world really wouldn't be so bad.
Then all that I see is not a true picture.
Lord, let me be paranoid so I know I'm not mad.

Dear God, my son prays for healthy paranoia concerning the social ills that he sees and feels as a young black person. I pray for holy restlessness and sensitivity to the racism that still affects the lives and impacts the aspirations of your children of the African sun. As we view human sin at work in the world, we pray for wisdom to discern that you created a good earth and that out of one blood you have made all nations to dwell upon the face of the earth.

As we fight the good fight of justice and righteousness against racism and other sins, we pray that we will keep before us the original intent of creation and that we will not replace old tyrannies with new ones. In the midst of our struggles help us to always be able to see beauty and your image in others who may be different from us.

We pray for passion regarding those things that ought not to be. Save us from complacency—the proverbial "I have arrived" syndrome—that cuts off our compassion and empathy for others who have not yet been able to overcome the battering they have received by sin and the vicissitudes of life. Deliver us from the temptation to shut ourselves up in our own little corner of the world, being content with whatever modicum of comfort and security we have been graced to achieve.

God, grant us sensitivity without cynicism, righteous indignation devoid of bitterness, the wisdom of the serpent without its craftiness, the gentleness of the dove without its naiveté. Then, Lord, help us to direct all of this passion that we feel into meaningful action, we pray. Amen.

To
Fall
in
Love

Two tiny leaves fell from a tree

The air teaching them to spin

Trickling down the maze of twigs

Being teased by the wind

Their twisted trails sometimes meeting

Only to part again

They twirled as if there were music playing

A timeless tune for them.

Thank you, God, for the chemistry between persons known as romantic love. Thank you, God, for your divine hand that guides us in our relationships with the myriad personalities with whom we interact, including the special ones in our lives.

Lord, we do not know the outcome of any of the relationships we nurture. We do know that one of the great joys in life is discovering love and joy, fulfillment and happiness in persons for whom there were no immediate fireworks when first we met. Sometimes, Lord, we wonder how we found the persons who put a new joy into our souls. Some may call such relationships of deep and abiding love "luck" or "fortuitous chance." But, God, we know that it was your hand that led us to the great loves of our lives. Thank you for leading us when we didn't know we were being led. Thank you for knowing us and our need to be loved. Thank you for giving to us such persons to bless our lives.

Now that you have helped us find each other, O God, hold us that we will not be tossed aimlessly about amid the cross winds of life like two drifting leaves. O God, teach us how to love each other that we might not take each other for granted or abuse each other or do things that are displeasing in your sight. Give to us a spirit of contentment that counteracts a wandering eye, a temptation to stray, and a curiosity that can kill.

In all ways and times we pray that our love for the special ones of our lives will glorify you. In Jesus' name, amen.

Dreams

The woman headed for the sign that said "Toys";
She was the mother of a little girl and boy.
She bought two bottles of bubbles, one pink, one blue
And told them that all their dreams would come true
If they put their fears inside the bubbles
Sending them to fly away until they were out of sight,
Then God would catch them and cast out their troubles
And everything would be all right.

Wishing away while watching the wind
Blow the bubbles farther away from them,
They would quickly work to make a new batch
Of iridescent globes that they would dispatch.
The girl and boy stood joyfully content
Feeling that their efforts were wisely spent.
As they launched the fragile spheres into the air
They wished and dreamed and hoped and shared.

The two continued for a real long time,
For a whole ten minutes that's all they did;
Instead of running around, they focused their minds
And that's pretty strange for little kids.
After a while the boy became very upset;
He pouted a bit and openly wept.
So the little girl asked him why he cried;
He told the girl that their mother had lied.

Since the bubbles would burst and fall to the ground
Just a few seconds after they were blown
Going no more than a couple of feet before dropping down
There was no way that God could know.
But the girl told him he was wrong,
That God hears our troubles—it doesn't take long
Before he is there to wipe our eyes,
To give us courage and make our spirits rise.

O God, how we need dreams! We need dreams to remind us of our possibilities. When we are confronted with failures and haunted by our inadequacies, when our sins expose our weaknesses and flaws in our characters—we need dreams to remind us of the untapped potential for goodness and nobility that you have placed within us. We need our dreams to draw us out of our selfishness and self-pity, out of mediocrity and low ambitions that we might have a taste for excellence and touch the extraordinary.

O God, we need dreams. All around us we see evidence of human insensitivity and cruelty. Every day we are victims of callous treatment by others. The news we read in papers, hear on radio, and see on television is burdensome to our spirits when we hear of the myriad forms of human violence. We need dreams of the great potential you have placed in others—even those whom we may regard as enemies and those whom we find it hard to love and impossible to like. Without a vision of the noble possibilities in others, we become captured by a denigrating cynicism and a self-defeating negativism.

O God, we need dreams. We need dreams for a better world. We need the messianic dreams of Isaiah. We need the remnant dreams of the prophets. We need the kingdom dreams of Jesus. We need the dreams of a new creation of John the revelator. We need dreams that give courage for the moment and hope for tomorrow. We need dreams that put joy into our spirits and love for life in our souls. We need dreams that put a song into our nights and a kiss of sunlight's golden ray on an otherwise dreary day. We need dreams that give us courage and make our spirits whole.

O God, we need dreams. O God, give us dreams. O God, help us not to lose our dreams, we pray. Amen.

Peepholes

walking down this hallway of life, I'm intrigued by many doors,
each having a peephole, each leading to a different destiny.
but peepholes have a way of distorting things so you can never be sure—
sure of what else is behind the door, what else you cannot see.

take the peephole of school—it seems like a waste of time
doing homework and studying when one could be having fun.
but what the peephole hides from your sight is the unemployment line—
the line that you'll be standing in without an education.

looking through the peepholes of sports I see money, fortune, and fame,
a life where I could live totally carefree.
but what the peephole hides from my sight is the big game—
the game where I shatter my career as I shatter my knee.

I reach the door of drugs, with its welcome mat and fancy doorknob,
and peeping I see people partying and encouraging me to knock.
but what you cannot see is them killing and robbing—
robbing their families, and anyone else, just for a small piece of the rock.

through the peephole of church you'll see an image of people devoting—
devoting their lives to God, though it doesn't seem to change a thing.
what the peephole hides from view is the angel who is noting—
noting their good deeds and good works to report to the king.

so always beware of peepholes; they can mislead the greatest of minds.
ask the sinner, the addict, the has-been, or the guy on the street;
they'll tell you to choose carefully the doors you enter or you'll find—
find that you've ruined your life for the sake of a peep.

O Lord, we need your Holy Spirit to guide us. There is so much in life that glitters like gold, but really isn't. Sin can be alluring and harmless in its appearance. We as humans can be foolish in our judgments, quick to err, mixed up in our priorities, insistent upon our own way, resistant to your will and word for our lives.

O God, we need your Holy Spirit to guide us, your Holy Presence to walk with us, your divine, sanctifying power to fill us. We need the power of the Holy Ghost to fall upon us that we might receive the gifts of wisdom and discernment regarding the doors that we ought to open and walk through and those that we should allow to remain shut as we pass them by. Give to us, we pray, the discipline not to look in places where we shouldn't and play with fire that can burn us.

O God, guide my son and others of his generation who have so many peepholes to look into—so many distractions, temptations, and opportunities to be led astray. We pray that amidst all the doors that they face, they may be led to the One who said, "I am the door; if any one enters by me, he will be saved, and will go in and out and find pasture."[3] In the name of that One, amen.

---

[3]John 10:9 (RSV)

Sunset

And the sun grew closer to the mountain
As I grew closer to you.
My heart welled over like the fountain
That filled the depths of my soul anew.

And the sun grew red and daring
As we grew to be of one accord.
Our growth and closeness were from sharing;
We shared without saying a word.

And the sun grew to be half under the earth
As we grew stronger in respect and trust,
Just as the seed holds tightly knowing the worth
Of all the riches held in the earth's crust.

And the sun grew to be no more,
All of its temperate rays now contained.
And though in the morn it would be restored,
Through the night our love remained.

O Lord, thank you for love in its morning stage. We praise you for the excitement we feel when the beat of our heart seems to pick up its pace because we've met someone who appeals to us in a special way. Thank you for the excitement we feel as we begin to explore mutual likes and dislikes, thoughts, and experiences, as we discover that what we suspected or hoped for at first is true—there is something special between us. Thank you for love in its morning stage that, like dew in the morn, puts a sparkle upon and refreshes our day.

Thank you for love at high noon. With the initial forays past, mutual interests confirmed, impressions made, and the first questions answered, thank you for love that has moved on to another stage, a deeper one. At this stage we dare to risk an argument, and we see that love is not all laughter, that the person who is the center of our romantic affection may have a flaw or two—and they discover the same about us. Yet our love holds and begins to grow deeper. Thank you, Lord. At noon the sun is midway in the sky, and in the summer it shines hottest; so for us passion is strong and the future seems brightest. Thank you, Lord, for love at high noon.

Thank you, Lord, for love at sunset. We've settled into each other without losing the freshness we first felt in the morning, and we've made some commitments to each other. We cannot imagine life without each other, and we're determined to make what we feel for each other work. Thank you, Lord, for love at sunset. We've had some ups and downs; we've cried as well as laughed together, and we look at life in similar, though not identical, ways. We know that what we have is irreplaceable, that it will last even when the sun goes down, and we praise you for life that would not have been complete for us had we not met and loved this particular person. Thank you for love at sunset that bestows tranquility upon our evenings, for love at sunset can be love at its sweetest.

Thank you, Lord, for love at sunset, for in such love we come closest to your love for us and ours for you. Amen.

Pressure

I've been doomed with potential all of my life;
Its danger is evident; it's very real.
This curse looms over me like a raised knife;
I see my reflection in the steel.
This curse was cast by my parents, my schools,
And all of the forces that shaped me.
They supplied all the motivation, the knowledge, and the tools,
The tools that doom me to seeking my destiny

Lord, we've tried to provide a good home for our children. We've tried to instill in them sound values and have encouraged them to strive for excellence. We have not told them what they should become or what to do with their lives or their futures. However, we have encouraged them to be persons of integrity and decency.

My son seems to feel burdened by his potential, and frankly, Lord, I'm at a loss. I've always believed that potential is a blessing to be explored, rather than a burden to be borne. All of us feel pressure, Lord. I remember the pressure I felt when I was young—pressure to live up to the expectations of others, pressure to do well in school, pressure to live up to my own expectations, pressure to do the right thing.

As my son comes to grips with what is pressure for him, I pray that he will come to understand that pressure can be an impetus as well as a weight. Pressure helps to keep us going. After all, automobile tires go flat without pressure. The pressure of competition brings out that last burst of energy within us that may otherwise lie dormant. Pressure can help us to grow.

Lord, rather than being relieved of pressure, may my son stay under the right kind of pressure—the pressure to grow to his fullest and reach for his highest as he pulls from the very depths of his being. May he never be content with that which is less that his best. But like the apostle Paul, may he press on toward the goal of the upward call of God in Christ Jesus. And as he presses on, I pray he will realize that he is not pursuing our expectations, but his own destiny under you. In Christ's name I pray, amen.

The Night

The night was long and the moon shone bright;
She and I walked til morning's light.
By morn we were far away;
We watched the clouds dance and play
In the sky like innocent kids
Still keeping the sun safely hid,
And by the time our walk was done
Our hearts had become as one.

O Lord, thank you for friendship and persons who genuinely love us, with whom we can dare to be ourselves and show our vulnerabilities. Thank you for those with whom we can have long conversations of substance as well as share lighthearted moments of laughter. Thank you for those with whom we can have long moonlit walks, those with whom we can watch clouds dance and play in the sky like innocent kids.

In this life, Lord, there is much duplicity, dishonesty, and hypocrisy. We often feel we have to keep our guard up when we meet people; we recognize that many persons have hidden agendas.

Thus, we are grateful for the blessing of relationships of trust, substance, mutual respect, genuine caring, common noble causes, shared values, and even a shared faith. We are grateful for those with whom our spirits can grow and our hearts beat as one, even when there are differences between us. We pray that we will never take lightly or misuse, abuse, dishonor, or betray any of those whom we are blessed to call friends—whether they be lifelong acquaintances, companions, parents, sisters, or brothers. For we learn from friends—who are blessings, living and incarnate—the meaning of love in all its aspects. Amen.

Glory

A boy sat on the bank of a river
Pitching pebbles in the morning sun
Watching the fragile water quiver,
Thinking of his life in years to come.

His mind focused on a single thought,
A question—what was the reason for his being?
The answer for which he so desperately sought
Remained out of his reach, constantly fleeing.

At times seeming ready to be captured
Only to slip away from his grasp,
Like a pebble escaping into the water
Leaving waves of confusion in its aftermath.

His mind deep in thought, he blindly stared
At the glare of the water; he sat unaware
That someone had approached his lonesome bank;
He sat totally still, his face was blank.

Then his silent world was pierced by a sound;
It was a voice, but the words he couldn't make clear.
He moved quickly from his place on the ground;
He saw no one there but he knew someone was near.

Catching hold of his senses he turned and peered
And saw an old man walk from around a tree trunk.
This was no old saint grown wise in his years;
The boy knew this man—he was the neighborhood drunk.

The boy was frightened by the tattered man
Who staggered onto the bank, with bottle in hand.
When the man looked up and saw someone there
He stumbled a step back; he also was scared.

Then the man stopped short in the middle of a word
In the song he was singing that the boy had heard;
And when each saw that the other was frightened
The moods changed and their faces brightened.

The two sat on the bank, the sun high in the sky;
They talked and laughed and even told stories.
The man had a strong laugh as he slapped his thigh,
And after a good long laugh he'd always shout, "Glory!"

The boy noticed this and decided to ask his friend
How he could be so happy and shout "glory" at the end
When the townspeople had treated him so coldly.
The man became serious, and after thinking said boldly,

"Everyone has always called me a drunken waste;
The townspeople labeled me a disgrace
Because I walk with a bottle and shout all the time.
I'm usually drunk, but it's not on their wine."

The man reached for his bottle and took off the top
And then poured out its contents drop by drop.
Out of the bottle came water to the boy's surprise
As the man laughed a bit and looked at the sky.

The sun started to set, taking back her warm touch
While the man explained why the water meant so much.
He told the boy with overflowing pride
That the water reminded him of when he got baptized.

But the boy still could not understand
Why this would bring so much joy to the man.
The boy innocently asked the man again
Why it brought so much happiness to him.

The man thought for a minute and picked up a stone
And tossed it lightly into the river.
He said, "Now the stone is no longer alone
Which is what happened to me when I got delivered.

I knew from then on that God was with me
And he has been with me until this very day,
Always keeping me in his arc of safety
And driving all my burdens swiftly away.

For he is with me, I know his presence;
I have heard him move; it sounds like peace,
It sounds like love, it sounds like joy;
It soothes my worries, it sings, it speaks

With a gentle voice of warm embrace
That softly puts my mind at ease
And fills my soul until it swells.
I hear his Spirit, I hear his peace,

For God is real; his presence bears fruit
That is ripe and nourishes all that eat.
I know his presence; I have heard him move;
I have tasted his fruit, and it is sweet.

For he is with me, I know his presence.
I have felt him move; it feels like joy,
It feels like peace, it feels like love,
It delights my mind, it drowns and destroys

All the contrary spirits that trouble my life;
My courage and strength it quickly employs
And brings confidence in my moments of weakness.
I feel his Spirit, I feel his joy.

For God is real; his presence bears fruit
That is ripe and nourishes all that eat.
I know his presence; I have felt him move;
I have tasted his fruit, and it is sweet.

God is with me, I know his presence.
I have seen him move; it looks like love,
It looks like joy, it looks like peace,
It surrounds my being, it seeks and shoves

Out all the cracks and flaws of my faith
In the One who sends blessings down from above
And shows me how much my God cares.
I see his Spirit, I see his love.

For God is real; his presence bears fruit
That is ripe and nourishes all that eat.
I know his presence; I have seen him move;
I have tasted his fruit and it is sweet."

The man was now standing, his hands on his hips,
His shoulders thrust back and fire on his lips.
And they say for miles around he could be heard
Proclaiming God's goodness with only one word—

A word that people had heard him yell every day
But never thought of it in this way.
It was a word that told his whole life story;
He held his head back and shouted, "Glory!"

O God, when I think about your goodness, your watchfulness, your faithfulness, your abiding presence, your protection, your grace and mercy, your forgiveness, and your patience—my soul within me shouts, "Glory!"

When I look back down the road over which I have come, the dangers seen and unseen that you have brought me through, the many times you have delivered me from the snares set by my own and others' foolishness—my soul within me shouts, "Glory!"

Whenever I stand upon a mountain crest or fly in an airplane and get a bird's-eye view of the beauty of your creation, when I think about innumerable forms of life found in the depths of the ocean—my soul within me shouts, "Glory!"

O God, thank you for the Holy Spirit who comforts and empowers, who rings joy bells in my soul, who helps me stand when I don't have strength to stand and helps me press on when doubts arise and fears dismay— "Glory!"

Thank you, God, for hearing my prayers and keeping your promises. Thank you for being my friend. Thank you for saving me. Thank you for calling me to preach your word. And now for the privilege of sharing this writing enterprise with my son, to see some of my prayers for him beginning to bear fruit, for his own experience of salvation—my soul within me shouts, "Glory!"

I love you, Lord—Glory! Amen.

Mighty Pollution

Scorched, scattered debris of life,
The product of innovation. Science is king;
Swollen lungs breathing laced air, wither and die;
The flesh of the earth writhes from the sting.

All hail, ruler, command us our fate;
Cast your will upon us, crush us with your weight;
Bind us and break us as we've given you this task;
We await your torture; we created your wrath.

O God, be merciful to us. We plead for mercy because mercy suits our case. We confess that in the development of our technology, which has often been fueled by the profit motive and our drive to master one another, we have created the means of our own destruction.

O God, help us to realize the seriousness of our situation— lest like those in the days of Noah, we eat and drink, buy and sell, plant and build until the floodwaters from the rising tide of our neglect overwhelm us; lest like those in the days of Lot, we eat and drink, buy and sell, plant and build until the fire of judgment from our own greed and callousness consumes us.

O God, create within us a clean heart and renew within us a righteous spirit. Perform divine surgery and remove our hearts of stone and replace them with hearts of flesh. We know that only renewed and new hearts, only hearts that put people over things, human life over political power, and our natural resources over profit, will work in conjunction with our minds, so that our knowledge will work for us, not against us, and that in all things we will glorify you.

Help us to understand that science is not king, but you are.

Amen.

I Grow Weary

I grow weary when I look ahead
At all of the road I still must tread,
My feet already feeling tired and worn,
Just from the few steps taken since I was born.

I grow weary when I look ahead,
Seeing all of the work before me; I begin to dread
My choice to be some kind of pioneer,
Losing my desire to pave some new frontier.

I grow weary when I look ahead
At all of the books that must be read,
At the sacrifices that I must make,
And wonder if I have made a mistake.

I grow weary when I look ahead
At the kind of lifestyle that must be led,
At the many words that must be said,
At the hungry mouths that must be fed.

I grow weary when I look ahead
At all that must be done before I'm dead.
I know there will also be happiness, but instead
I grow weary when I look ahead.

O God, we all sometimes feel overwhelmed when we look at the road that lies ahead, the distance that must yet be covered, the tasks that must be done, the obstacles and difficulties that await us, and the burdens that must yet be borne. Sometimes, Lord, the road stretches so far into the horizon that we become weary before we start.

In those times of our feeling overwhelmed, speak to us, Lord. Help us remember that we do not travel distance all at one time, but step by step, day by day, hour by hour, and minute by minute and that we walk by faith, not by sight. As we face what is ahead, give to us a sense of priority and proper ordering so that we will keep the responsibilities of life and our own strength and abilities in proper focus.

We pray, dear God, that we will always keep you in focus, for you are the One who gives us strength for the journey. With you we have joy on our journey. When we have the joy of the Lord as our strength, we bring a positive spirit to the tasks we face, transforming them from burdens to blessings.

When we become weary we pray for faith that turns to you and remembers your word: "Even youths will faint and be weary, and the young will fall exhausted: but those who wait for the LORD shall renew their strength, they shall mount up with wings like eagles, they shall run and not be weary, they shall walk and not faint."[4]

To you, O God who gives strength for the journey, we commit our way and our walking. Amen.

---

[4]Isaiah 40:30-31 (NRSVB)

One of
Those
Days

Yesterday I woke up and got out of bed;
    I was not looking and I hit my head.

I went to school and like a fool
    I wasn't looking and tripped over a stool.

I went to Burger King 'cause I had a hunger attack,
    But by mistake I ordered a Big Mac.

I came home in a daze
    And decided it was
    Just one of those days.

O Lord, we all have those days—those days when nothing seems to go right, those days that are unproductive, characterized by a dulling sameness without anything of significance or noteworthiness happening in our lives. We all have those no-growth, plateau days that make us question the what and why of our actions and sometimes of life itself.

Help us during those days to remember that every day is a blessed day. Every day is a day that you have made wherein we can rejoice and be glad for life itself and for blessings that we sometimes take for granted, such as health and strength, family and friends, a sound mind, and a faith that dares to hope.

Help us in moments of mediocrity, during "blah" days, to remember the preciousness of life and to see opportunities for growth and service that are always around us. Save us from self-pity, Lord. And in the midst of life, help us not to take ourselves too seriously.

Give to us a sense of humor that helps us laugh, even at ourselves, and then determination to keep on living and striving until our defeats become our victories. Amen.

Thanks for the rain

as the puddles danced i was engulfed in pain;
the source of my affliction was the piercing rain.
you created the rain when you left me that day;
i saw no flowers in the month of May.

now August has come, the summer was dry,
and looking back on it all, i understand why.
you left and said you were leaving for me;
it was because you saw something i could not see.

these past few months i've been doing some changing;
i saw that i needed to do some rearranging.
i thought you didn't love me when you walked out the door;
now i realize you couldn't have loved me more.

rain is needed in order for things to grow;
you turned into that rain when you decided to go.

O Lord, we praise you for your goodness that has placed within our experiences many opportunities for growth. We recognize growth to be a characteristic of life and a blessing from you. Sometimes, Lord, we would abide in zones of comfort and have things remain the same. However, you have built growth and change into this world of living beings. Thank you, Lord, for growth moves us to full maturity, whereas sameness, no matter how comforting and comfortable it is, can lead to stagnation and atrophy. Thank you, Lord, for willing and then making possible our full maturity as unique specimens of your living creativity through the process we know as growth.

O God, sometimes we must confess that we are frightened by growth because we don't know what changes will take place as we grow. We aren't sure what we will be like, what others will look like, how life will appear, and how we will perceive institutions and things that we hold dear.

And sometimes, Lord, we are afraid to grow because growth can be painful. New knowledge and maturity can be painful. They can debunk cherished illusions, dethrone beloved idols, and cause us to shed our naiveté even as the butterfly leaves the safe cocoon behind so that it can spread its wings and fly.

Sometimes, Lord, as my son has experienced, you help us to grow through persons who are special to us and through human relationships that hold pain as well as pleasure.

We pray for faith to trust you and wisdom to know that all things still work together for good to those who love you, who are called according to your purpose. Give us hearts that respond to your love even in the midst of life's piercing rain, which helps us to grow.

In Jesus' name, amen.

Faith

I don't know what the future holds for me,
But I do know who holds my destiny.
There are many things I don't understand
That will be revealed as part of life's plan.
There is One who comes from above,
Whose heart is filled with pure love.
He gives me guidance and answers prayers;
He does all this because he cares.
Now I know where my health comes from,
And if he calls me I will surely come,
For it is in him that I keep my faith.

Lord, none of us knows what the future holds, but we are eternally grateful that we know you, for you hold all of our tomorrows even as you held all of our yesterdays—yea, even as you hold us this present moment—in your hands.

Gracious God, we come before you with thanksgiving that our son is developing his own relationship with you. We pray that your Holy Spirit will guide him and that he may come to know and love you as heavenly parent and faithful friend. O God, we pray that he will have discernment to know your will and courage to follow your will for his life. Keep him, dear God, even as Jesus prayed that you would keep the disciples and the church.

Now, Lord, help us as parents to live a life before our son that will not deter, but encourage, his interest in spirituality. When he comes to us with questions of faith, we pray that you will help us guide him aright and answer appropriately and correctly. May he see in our lives examples of faith, commitment, and loving trust that will inspire him to draw close to you as well as deeper in you.

As the running deer pants for the cool refreshment of the babbling brook, may his heart, soul, and spirit thirst for you, the Living God. Amen.

EVOLUTION

Borne to this country with our feet in chains,
Adorned with whip marks and bruises from canes,
Torn from our homeland, torn from our kin,
Scorned for our gift of darkened skin.

Sticks answering the protesters' cries,
Bricks in the air, gas in our eyes.
Kicked by a cop, the woman fell down,
Picked by the hose, he was knocked to the ground.

Caught in a life of pain with no relief,
Brought to the point of being filled with grief.
Wrought with a vengeance that runs down to the bone,
Taught only to carry it out on our own.

God, we are a people who have come over a way that with tears has been watered. However, through it all we have made it; your power has brought us through. We praise you and adore you, O God, that your power has been greater than any of the obstacles and adversities that have been raised against us.

Sometimes, God, we must confess that historically, and all too often in the present, we take the frustrations caused by the onerous burden of racism out on one another. Perhaps we do so because at times we have bought into the system that denies self-worth, that fosters self-hate. Sometimes we have turned upon one another because we have felt impotent and unable to reach the real enemy. It is easier to strike down an ethnic sister or brother than to tackle systemic racism and its living, visible symbols and representatives.

Redirect our attention and energies, O God. Give to us the guidance of the Holy Spirit so that we will stay focused in the struggle. Give to us the comfort of the Holy Spirit that we might fight bitterness and refrain from turning upon one another. Give to us the power of the Holy Spirit that we might continue in the struggle.

We pray for the power of our resurrected Lord, whose example has shown us the triumphant power of love and righteousness when they are rooted in the Truth that you are.

At all times, in our most despairing, discouraging, and bewildering moments, when striking out at those closest to us becomes easiest, we pray that we remember that you have not brought us this far to leave us and that you have promised inheritance of all things to those who remain faithful to the tasks at hand. Amen.

The Past,
the Present,
or the Future?

I had a bizarre dream one
stormy night in May.
I tossed and turned as I lay
Dreaming of this nation's decay.

As I watched the dream go by,
I could not help but wonder why
Some rich people cheat and lie
And why poor people starve and die.

Lord, there are many questions I cannot answer for my son regarding social inequities. Lord, you know I have my own set of questions that perplex me. Like Jeremiah of old, as a black American Christian, I also wonder why the lot of black people is such a hard one. Why is it that whenever the city of freedom comes either within sight or in striking distance, it eludes us, or a mist rolls in and it is lost again from view?

What's going to happen to our race, particularly our youth? What about the vanishing black male? What about apartheid in South Africa? Will black people ever be free? Will we ever have the privilege of sitting under our own vine and fig tree of peace and justice? Will we ever know what it is like not to study war anymore? Why can't we come into our own as other people seem to do? Or will the blackness that you have given us as our unique gift be forever used by others as a weapon against us—a reason for hating us or holding us down?

I thank you, Lord, for faith that keeps my soul centered and my spirit intact in the midst of these baffling questions. I thank you for faith that teaches me my inherent worth as your child and as your creation, irrespective of the assaults of western culture and the policies and politics of international racism.

I thank you, God, especially for a son who feels deeply and cares greatly about justice questions, for it is in asking questions that we are motivated to action. May he find in you solace and strength for his struggles, both personal and social. Keep, I pray, his mind alert, his soul enlarged, his heart filled with compassion, and his spirit free from bitterness. In Jesus' name, amen!

It Is Too Late

A token marriage and lovely lies
All because they couldn't wait.
A broken carriage and the baby cries;
All is lost, it is too late.

An open door and mother grieves
All because they couldn't wait.
She is alone as father leaves,
And all is lost, it is too late.

Lost dreams and hollow lives
All because they couldn't wait.
Quiet screams and shallow eyes;
All is lost, it is too late.

O God, we've made many mistakes—devastating mistakes, foolish mistakes, mistakes from ignorance, mistakes from impertinence, mistakes from impetuousness. There is much we would do differently if we could live our lives all over again. However, our past is our past, and we cannot change it. No matter how much we weep over the bygone days that have brought us into our stormy present, there is nothing we can do to change our history; it is too late.

But, O God, we praise you for the gospel of redemption that tells us our past does not have to determine our future. No matter what we've left undone in the past, the future stands before us offering unlimited possibilities, because for your children it stretches into eternity.

O God, create in us clean hearts and new spirits. We pray that we might be born anew in Christ Jesus, so that we can face the future with new vision, new zeal, new determination, and new hands with which we will build tomorrows that will far surpass prospects that those who looked at our past thought possible.

O God, give us the urgency of now, for if the future is to be saved, we must begin redeeming it today. So God, we pray that this very day we may quit weeping over the past for which it is too late and begin working on the future that we have in our grasp.

We pray this in the name of Jesus Christ our Lord, who redeems us from our past mistakes and guilt so that we can live fully in the present and lay claim to the future. Amen.

Two Men

In this land of hate and sin
There lived two men of great power.
Their power came from within,
Yet they were gentle as a flower.
They contributed their lives to the nation.
To them equality was a treasured thing;
Their devotion was beyond calculation.
Their names—Malcom X and Martin Luther King.

O God, thank you for Malcolm and Martin-two who represented the strength, dignity, and enduring courage of black manhood.

O God, thank you for Malcolm and Martin-two who were not ashamed to affirm their faith tradition and who lived the faith they affirmed.

O God, thank you for Malcolm and Martin-two who were devoted to the liberation of your people, both the oppressed and the oppressor.

O God, thank you for Malcolm and Martin-two in whom we recognized your Spirit of truth as they constantly sought your will and your face.

We praise you for their refusal to bow before golden images of mediocrity and compromise. We praise you for their unflinching fortitude as they walked through the fire of false accusation and misrepresentation. We praise you for their passion for justice as well as their compassion for all. We praise you for their ever-expanding vision and their continuing deepening in you.

We thank you for role models such as these. May our commitment to justice and principle be as uncompromising as theirs. We pray that we may rededicate ourselves anew here and now to the struggle against principalities and powers as reflected in the quest for peace and justice and justice with peace for which they died.

O God, thank you for Malcolm and Martin. Amen.

She

She moves in slow rhythmic motion;
The green sways gently like the ocean,
The brown stays firm and never tires.
She only has a fear of fire.
She is too strong to be made to fall
And she is much too wide and much too tall.
But one day a blackness rolls in on the air;
Her beauty is diminished from wonderful to fair.
She can no longer hold her head up high;
Now people stare and wonder why.
She would still be able to stand
If it had not been for poisons that should have been banned.
The people finally find the solution;
Her murderer was their pollution.
She is now only a shell of what she used to be;
They themselves killed this mighty tree.

O Lord, our Lord, how excellent is your name in all the earth. You have taught us that the earth is yours and the fullness thereof, the world and they that dwell therein, and you have committed the earth to our care and keeping.

We acknowledge our failures as responsible stewards of your *oikoumene*—your whole inhabited earth. Too often we have limited our stewardship to our families and friends, our neighborhoods or towns, states or regions, nations or races, or even to other human beings. Help us to realize that we must be concerned about all of the earth—the animals and insects, fish and fowl, rocks and rivers, plants and trees—all of which represent your fullness.

Teach us to be sensitive to the ways that our creature comforts, arrogance, sectionalism, political differences, and senseless wars impact upon your creation and the place of our habitation. Your bountiful hand has provided all that we need. We pray for wisdom to take care of the natural resources given to us so that the firmament will continue to declare your glory and the heavens show forth your handiwork. Amen.

The Drug Wars

Speak up soldiers, now what do you lack?
Let us finish preparing for our greatest attack.
Sir, I need more bullets, a knife, and canteen.
I used most of my bullets and left the knife in his spleen;
My canteen was damaged; can my order be filled?
Certainly, Private, for the many you've killed.

Speak up, soldiers, now what do you lack?
Let us finish preparing for our greatest attack.
Sir, I lost my compass and some of my rations;
Though I did not kill many, I'm filled with a passion.
Private, I'll reissue your losses; I admire your drive;
Maybe next time the enemy will not survive.

Speak up, soldiers, now what do you lack?
Let us finish preparing for our greatest attack.
If no one else is in need of supplies—on to the next subject at hand,
That of recruiting soldiers for our terrible band.
You'll find the poorer ones are easy to lure.
The promise of gold will get them for sure.

The next subject of discussion is our plan of attack.
We'll let the poor ones kill their own while we wait in the back.
Then, when their task is just about done,
We'll have reinforcements to make them succumb.
Now, soldiers, do you have any last-minute questions?
Sir, won't the government give them protection?

Soldier, how do you think we've gotten this far?
We wouldn't have made it if the door wasn't ajar.
They are our secret weapon, our ace in the hole;
It's because of them that we'll reach our goal.
Now, soldiers, if there is nothing you lack,
Let us begin our greatest attack!

O God, how do we—how *dare* we—stand up against evil when like cobwebs, it is found in unreachable, unobserved, and unsuspected places? Evil is so powerful and has such massive weaponry, such a large army with crafty and vicious generals, and such an extensive underground counter-intelligence network that we sometimes feel overwhelmed and ask ourselves, "Where do we begin? What can we do?" Your Holy Word has reminded us that "we are not contending against flesh and blood, but against principalities, against powers, against the world rulers of this present darkness, against the spiritual hosts of wickedness in the heavenly places." However, your Word also instructs us to "take the whole armor of God, that [we] may be able to withstand in the evil day, and having done all to stand." [5]

In moments when we feel overwhelmed and discouraged, we pray that we would remember that we, too, have weapons. We have truth that will not bow, righteousness that will not bend, a gospel of peace that liberates as it reconciles, the reality of salvation, God's unconquerable Word, and prayer that unleashes the Power that created the universe. We praise you that we have a general—even Jesus Christ our Lord, the captain of the Lord's host. We praise you that we have an intelligence network—the Holy Spirit.

We pray that we remember we do not fight alone or stand by ourselves. As you were with Moses and Joshua, Deborah and Esther, Elijah and Daniel, and Paul and Silas, as you were with Jesus, so you are and will continue to be with us.

God, the plague of drugs is destroying our land. There is hardly a family that has escaped the touch of this latter-day death angel. A number of our political leaders and even some of our law enforcement officials do not know whether to continue fighting or legalize yet another vice and destructive force among us.

Almighty God, grant us courage so that we will continue resisting the beast in our midst, even when it is found in high places. We take comfort in knowing that a higher power in a higher place not only reaches down, but also walks with us in life's lowlands of struggle.

---

[5]Ephesians 6:12-13 (KJV)

Run Away

I run away from things that are bad,
Things that scare me or make me sad;
I run away from the poison of hate.
For some adults it is too late.
They do not know the gift of love;
They can't see what comes from above;
They are blind and so they wait
Just for another chance to hate.
One day I know that hate will be gone
And harsh words and bickering will change to song,
But til that day I'll continue to run—
Until that new day has begun.

O God, we feel like running away sometimes. At times we all wish we had wings like a dove so we could fly away and be at rest. There are times when we all wish for some wayside lodge where we might leave the violence and the hatred that we see.

O God, hatred can be such a baffling phenomenon to young people who have been taught that God loves them and that they are just as good as anybody else.

O God, I pray that those of us who are prototypes, examples, and major shapers of the perspectives of younger people, will not pass on to them bitterness, cynicism, or the same prejudices that have been imposed on us.

O God, I especially pray that we will not pass on fear. Help my son and others like him not to be afraid—afraid to face life with all of its inconsistencies, challenges, and problems; afraid that some nuclear holocaust will cut off their future. Help my son and other young people to stand firm and fight for what they believe in—for truth and justice, a better world, and a brighter tomorrow. Help them to stand firm in you and to know that because you are both a just and an all-powerful God who wills righteousness and peace, our efforts will not be in vain when we devote our lives to noble causes and strive for justice, peace, and the integrity of the creation. Amen.

Just a Dance

With a check of my breath and a smile on my face
I headed toward her, walking with grace.
Then my thoughts became jumbled up in my brain
And all of my smooth lines went right down the drain.

My confident stride lost all of its glide;
As I got closer, I quivered inside.
Mustering an unknown courage I took the chance
And with a cracking voice I asked her to dance.

I almost fainted when she said yes
And cursed my tongue for getting me into this mess.
My knees felt weak and I could not speak;
To quote a phrase, I was up the creek.

But then she smiled, which calmed my nerves,
And I decided to let my actions replace my words.
So with grace and charm I started to dance.
Yep, you guessed it—I slipped and fell and ripped my pants.

God, are you laughing with us? Not mocking or ridiculing us, not laughing at us, not shaking your head or groaning over your creation—but are you laughing with us? We hope so, Lord, because we could feel so much closer to you if we knew that the gift of humor and laughter that you have anointed us with, like the attributes of freedom and love, are found in you as they are found in us.

God, if you are the quintessence of holiness and the first and greatest love and the originator of freedom, then you must also be the creator of laughter. One can't give what one doesn't have, and so, God, you must really have an almighty sense of humor.

There is often much formalism between us, and because of our sins there is often distance between us. Because you are infinite, my finite mind cannot grasp the mysterious ways of divine providence. And so, Lord, sometimes there are questions between us.

God, I praise you for this moment of revelation that your ever-creative Spirit has given me, that lets me see a bit more of your character and lets me know that you have a sense of humor. What is any genuine, living relationship without humor and laughter but something that is drab and lifeless? And since we have such a close, loving relationship, there has to be laughter and humor between us.

So laugh with us, Lord, I pray. Laugh with us when we're trying to make great impressions and end up looking foolish and must laugh at ourselves. Laugh with us, Lord, when we're trying to be something we're not and end up revealing ourselves as we are—uniquely created human "klutzes." Laugh with us, Lord, when we try to do either great or simple tasks and seem to be all thumbs, or try to take great and simple steps and stumble over our feet, or try to make eloquent or ordinary speeches and fumble over our words. When we just can't seem to get it all together or keep it together and must laugh at ourselves, won't you please share those moments with us and laugh with us, Lord? Amen.

Behold Thy Mother

When I look up at the sky on a sunny day
I can see my mother in a way,
Not as the sun, but as the steamy shroud
Around the sun—the lovely cloud.
Notice the way she changes shape
Offering herself to the sun as a peaceful escape.
Ofttimes she has conformed herself to me
To comfort the pain which only she could see.
I see her resting at her heavenly height;
I see her twirls and curls so pearly white.
She sits far above the cheapness of the earth.
She has been kind and loving to me since birth.

When I look up at the sky on a rainy day
I can see my mother in a way,
Not as a droplet of rain, but in the form
Of the rain cloud in the raging storm,
For in this cloud has been placed lightning and thunder
By the same Being who has given her such a powerful essence
To cast down her love on all that are under
The shadow of her striking presence.
I see her floating vast and dark;
She is above the reach of the strongest lark.
I see her send nourishment from above
As she floods my life with her endless love.

I can see my mother on that last day,
The angels preparing Yahweh's way,
Their trumpets calling clear and loud
As he comes to collect his dearest cloud,
Setting her soul free from its misty case,
Showing her the eternal resting place,
Raising her high above his chest,
Placing her atop heaven's crest
So all can see my mother the way that I
See her when I look up at the sky.

O God, I praise you for my wife and my son's mother. I thank you for her love and devotion expressed in quiet, yet influential ways. When I was away from home making a living, she was at home making lives. When I was on the road traveling, she was at home maintaining discipline. After I had propounded values from the pulpit, she lived those values and taught them to our children. O God, I thank you for my companion and Matthew's mother.

Sometimes, Lord, it seemed as if our teachings went unheeded and our advice was for naught. Now as our children mature, we are grateful that much of what we have tried to sow in faith is taking root and we await with hope the harvest.

There were times, Lord, when tension developed between mother and son, between one generation and another, between mother's love that pressed and prayed for the best out of her son and a young African American male's determination to be independent. There were times when my son didn't understand all that his mother and father were trying to instill in him. There were times when he rebelled against the discipline of love that would not abide or tolerate mediocrity.

I don't know if Matthew fully comprehends all that his mother and I have tried to teach him. However, I am grateful that he has reached a point in his life where he can begin to appreciate, honor, and affirm his mother, even though he may not always understand her (or me either, for that matter). I am truly grateful that he is able to look back and recognize that on both sunny and rainy days, through piercing heat and lightning and thunder, his mother has always been there for him—and that her love is as magnificent as the sky and her capacity to give is as great as the breadth of the clouds and that her faith qualifies her to receive a hearty "well done" from her Lord whom she loves as she does her family. O God, thank you for Muriel, my companion of twenty-three years and Matthew and Jennifer's mother. Amen.

The
Field

As we walked together hand in hand
Making patterns in the sand,
My heart sang a song of love
Of her, my precious, gentle dove.
The field moved gently like a wave
Much like her hair that special day,
And when we kissed at that time
I knew at that moment she was mine.
I would give anything to be there again
Back in the field with the wind.

Thank you, Lord, for special moments with special people. Amidst all of the mundane striving for things that do not satisfy, amidst all of the turmoil and strife around us, thank you, Lord, for quiet moments and special times with special people.

Lord, my son is at that age when he is discovering the joys of female companionship. As I look back across the years, I remember with fondness the excitement of being attracted rather than repelled by members of the opposite sex. I do not remember having at my son's age the conscious sense of the romantic or the gift of poetic expression to help me articulate my feelings. If I had the gift, I did not use it.

Lord, thank you for the romantic spirit in my son's soul. Thank you for the courage that you have given him to be unashamed in expressing his feelings of romance and compassion. I pray that as he builds relationships with young ladies, he will respect them for their inner qualities and that old chauvinistic ideas still prevalent in my generation will be absent from his love.

Give him strength for his tenderness and tenderness for his strength, I pray. Amen.

Jennifer, My Sister

The worth of your friendship cannot be reflected in words,
For words cannot express its value to me.
To attempt to pay homage with money is absurd,
For there is not enough money to pay homage to thee.

Because of your love of God, family, and self
You have acquired friendships that are meaningful and true.
You shall always be rich, regardless of wealth,
Because your friends, family, and God will be there for you.

I pray God's blessing in the pursuit of your dreams,
And that your actions will continue to be pleasing in God's sight,
Always realizing that the end does not justify the means,
So that the success you gain is from doing what's right.

I love you for the way you have helped me to grow,
Giving me the guidance that I need in times of despair,
For explaining to me things I didn't know;
I love you simply for the way that you care.

Truly you are a young woman of promise and virtue;
Truly you possess many keys to success.
These keys will open doors through which you may enter;
The most important key is that you realize you're blessed.

O God, you have blessed my life with two wonderful children, and I praise you for them. I thank you for a companion who has labored to instill within them noble values. I praise you for the promise of each of their lives, and I pray that Muriel and I will continue to be guided by you as we endeavor to guide them.

I come to you now, dear God, to praise you for the love that my children have for each other. Not only do they love each other, they like, affirm, respect, and trust each other. Not every brother would praise his sister in a poem. So for such a love that expresses itself in such a way, I praise you.

Lord, you know our family is like any other family—we have our moments of tension, frustration, and disappointment. You know that Jennifer and Matthew are like any other brother and sister—they have their moments of sibling rivalry, confrontation, and conflict. However, as they mature into young adulthood, I am so grateful that they are putting many childish attitudes behind them and are seeing qualities of nobility worthy of emulation in each other.

As they move, ever so swiftly it seems, into maturity, I pray that they will continue to grow closer to each other. I pray for their friendship as well as their family ties.

You who are Father and Mother, Sister and Brother to each of us, grant them your peace. In Jesus' name, amen.

RAGE

I am consumed by a rage I've never before known.
I do not fight its power; instead I feed.
It quickly turns my soul to stone,
My hardened heart refuses need.

This rage ignites in me a fierce desire
To hurt, to maim, at any cost.
It engulfs me, growing stronger and higher,
And I am now completely lost.

It shuns my feelings, it shuns my fears.
I lash out as a rabid hound,
Attacking anyone who would draw near,
Their horrid cries to me a bittersweet sound.

O God, control our rage. All of us sometimes feel as if we are about to explode. Small, irritating incidents and incessant problems have a way of driving us to the wall, making us feel harried and boxed in. Sometimes we become so filled with the stuff of life, with our anger at personal and social injustice, and even with people, that we just want to scream or strike out in desperation as we try to relieve the pressure.

O God, control our rage. Control the rage, we pray, of young people. They, like those of us who are further along in years, have their own concerns, fears, frustrations, and problems. Give to us who are older adults listening ears, understanding hearts, and sensitive spirits, so that we might truly hear what they say to us and truly feel their pain. Give us wisdom that we might guide them from anger to productive activity.

Don't take away our rage; help us to control our rage, so that the passion we feel will be a blessing rather than a bane. When we feel pushed to the limit, we pray that you would:

> Drop Thy still dews of quietness,
> Till all our strivings cease;
> Take from our souls the strain and stress,
> And let our ordered lives confess
> The beauty of Thy peace.[6]

O God, control our rage. Amen.

---

[6]From "Dear Lord and Father of Mankind," by John Greenleaf Whittier.

My Never Love

I share a thought a fleeting hope
Of moments not to be real
And hollow out within my soul
A place where they may lie still
Where they may be covered in a peace
One too deep to be moved
Leaving me whole and strong
Allowing my heart to be soothed.

O God, help us to live with the unfulfilled. You are caring enough to provide for all of our needs and gracious enough to give us some of our wants. You are compassionate enough to provide us with what we stand in need of before we ask or when we fail to ask. And you are loving and understanding enough to bless us even when we fail to say thank you. Your throne is always open to us and your mercy seat is always available to us. You always hear our faintest cry, and you are diligent to answer every heartfelt prayer—sometimes with yes, sometimes with no, and sometimes with wait.

Yet God, you and I both know that there are desires in our hearts that will not become realities. Some of those desires, Lord, we dare not share with anyone—but they are there and you know it. Some of them we shouldn't have because there is a course unto a person that seems right but the end leads to destruction. Some of them we can't have because they belong to another, and we know, God, that you will not harm another one of your children or break their hearts just to bless us. And some of them, God, are all right; they do not belong to another, and they would not draw us away from a sacred nearness to you—they are just not meant for us. They are not meant to be.

O God, help us to live with the reality of the unfulfilled. Help us not to be resentful of others who have what we desire. Help us not to resent you when you have something for us that is different from our secret fantasy or wish. Help us always to be grateful for the many ways in which you choose to bless us. Help us to be at peace with your decisions about what we should have and shouldn't have.

In Jesus' name do we pray, amen.

My Utopian Existence

Of time traveled and distance captured
Of plains of beauty my soul is enraptured,
Of delicate figures within the scheme
All of which flower within my dream,

Spacious and lovely; I sit and bask
In the reverence and presence of the past
Amidst wondering hues of soft pastels
But as crisp as the chime of a bell.

Happily, I rest and feast
Upon the pleasures that lie within my reach,
The flowing colors, the sounds so gay,
The warm air caresses me as I lay.

My mind melts and melds my mystic muse
Mixing the magical sensations until they fuse
Into ample waves of pleasure manifold
That rise and fall and make me whole.

O God, I am grateful that my son can write about utopia. Amidst reflections about racism, drugs, pollution, and death, I'm grateful that my son's world view is balanced by some utopias.

Utopias really do help us attain wholeness. Often in our sterile, empirical, matter-of-fact world we sometimes regard utopias as a precious waste of time and energy, as fools' paradises, as fruitless jousting at windmills. However, without utopias, without a heaven in our view, we easily fall prey to a pessimism that is neither sane, realistic, nor wholesome. Without utopias, we can too easily fall into the fallacious thinking that what we see is all that there is to reality. Without utopias, we can easily lose hope, and without hope we are most miserable and most weak.

And so, God, thank you for utopias, and although I do not understand all that my son sees and says about his utopia, I am grateful that he has one— that he is able to dream dreams without making dreams his master and think thoughts without making thoughts his aim. Give us the gift of a balanced faith that allows us to be both romanticists and realists and to view the ugly without losing our perspective of utopia. Amen.

Domination

Man of dust, swept from earth
Tempered in her fiery girth
Cooled by the milk of her breast
Refined and gently laid to rest.

Inside a plush, a tender cradle
He slept soundly, without dismay.
She sent a cloud, her misty ladle
To awaken him from where he lay.

Born a full man, his back already strong,
His nose already wide, his legs already long,
His mind sharp and keen, his skin a blackened sheen,
He rose up to find his beautiful African queen.

She a stellar seed sown in sacred soil
Toiled with the dirt causing it to roil.
Her thirst was quenched by a nourishing shower;
She opened her petals to reveal heaven's flower.

Upon sun-whitened sand she stood tall and proud,
Strong and regal with her head properly endowed
With the only crown worthy of resting upon her spire,
Her black kinky hair reflecting the complexity of her desire.

Her legs lifted her torso like a sculpture being exhibited.
The power of her character could not be inhibited.
This force emanating from her could not be denied
For God was the source that had placed it inside.

She carried herself in a manner that demanded respect
That stemmed from the high caliber of her intellect.
Then she strode forth in search of only one thing,
A man of the same glorious ilk—her handsome African king.

A nexus of honor was reached at the initial meeting;
He bowed a knee, extending his greeting;
She expected his action and extended her hand
As he kissed it and rose before her, to stand.

Many times the sun and moon crossed the sky
As the passing time went by,
As they talked and shared, it seemed
As if they were living a dream.

Each having been crowned by the same entity—
The Creator and Shaper of antiquity,
God who granted them the kingdom over which they would reign;
The entire breadth of the land and sea was within their domain.

Yet their growing came to a sudden halt
With each of their strong wills trying to exalt
Itself to a place where it could dictate
The course of the relationship and its fate.

He felt that because he was a man
It was his place to be the boss;
But when he made his defiant stand
She became enraged and very cross.

For she felt it was her inherent role
To direct him and take control
Of his will and their affairs,
But he refused and his temper flared.

The land became unsettled, the sky was gray,
The sea was troubled, all was in disarray.
Chaos filled the air all around;
Not knowing what to do they dropped to the ground.

He was a man formed from the dust,
She was a woman who blossomed from heaven's seed.
Their combating wills became still
As both found themselves on their knees.

They realized there was power greater than their own.
Then they understood that one could not grow alone,
For even when a seed is planted in the earth,
Without the workings of God, there would be no growth.

They found that they would not be hindered
If either decided to surrender,
And that dominance belonged to neither gender
For love does not conquer—true love renders.

Each abandoned individual intentions
And assumed proper roles in humble submission
To show proper praise to God's divine presence
With earnestness, reverence, devotion, and deference.

O God, you have made all of us in your image; forgive us for our spirit of domination. When we use our differing endowments of talents and gifts as a reason for feeling superior, forgive us, O God. When we use our gender differences and respective physical capabilities as a rationale for dominance, forgive us, O God. When we use our distinct skin tones and ethnicity as an excuse to hate, forgive us, O God. When we use the proportion of your bounty entrusted into our hands as a means to oppress others, forgive us, O God. When we use our various approaches to you, our differing understandings and ways of talking about and experiencing you to legitimate division and suspicion in the human family, forgive us, O God. When we view as inferior differences that are hallowed and blessed by you, forgive us, O God.

Forgive us for our spirit of domination, O God, particularly felt by me in my own community and among my African American brothers and sisters. As we come into our own as females and males, help us to lay aside old patterns of oppression and suppression that we may be born anew in a spirit of mutual respect that honors a God in whose sight we are equals.

O God, we pray that among the sons and daughters of Africa, competition will be replaced by cooperation, that suppression will be replaced by mutual support, antagonism will give way to affirmation, domination to devotion, division to dialogue, conquest to conscientiousness, and haughtiness to humility.

Amen.

Taking
a
Stand

G'on to the back of the bus, Boy—you know where you belong.
You been riding this bus all your life; you know that you are wrong.
Now don't try to get loud and cause a scene
Just 'cause you following that Martin Luther King.
I'll call the cops, and then you'll feel
The white man's mighty hand of steel.
We've known each other for a real long time,
Your kids used to play with mine.
So think of them in your haste;
Leaving them with no father would be a waste.
Do me a favor and go to the back of the bus;
Ain't ya'll learned you can't whip us?

O God, as a black man, I get exceedingly tired and so filled up with confronting and fighting racism, that formidable foe. It passes its poison from one generation to another. It has polluted all of the wellsprings of the nation's institutional life. More widespread than the drug scourge, more explosive than nuclear weapons, more crippling than germ warfare—racism has washed up on the shores of every nation of every continent.

O God, I get so tired of racism wherever I go—abroad and at home. From stores that let me know that I have gotten "out of place"; from looks of fear that my black manly presence engenders in some; from small insults to major offenses; from polite, subtle, condescending paternalism or maternalism to outright, open hostility; from insulting jokes about my intelligence to curiosity about alleged black sexual prowess; from caricatures and stereotypes to the "you are the exception" syndrome—racism rears its many heads and shows its various faces all the time.

Yet as I bow before you, O God, I pledge to you, to my ancestors who sacrificed greatly so that I might enjoy whatever rights and privileges—however limited or circumscribed—are mine to experience, and to my children and to their children that I will keep up the noble fight of faith and perseverance. I will not go back to the back of the bus. I will not accept the invincibility of racism and the inviolability of its mythical sacred precepts.

I know that greater is the One that is in me than the one that is in the world. May that Spirit's presence and power direct and inspire me now and evermore until victory is won for my people, and all people, and until the kingdoms of this world become the kingdom of our Lord and of his Christ. Amen.

Different Paths

He felt that scholarship would be the best way

To help his people out of the ruins and decay,

While another man felt that vocation

Was the answer for blacks in this nation.

Each man would help his race

And in history would find his place.

We find that both men made the right choice;

They were Booker T. Washington and W.E.B. Dubois.

O God, thank you for raising up leaders for us. As we your children of the African sun have endured, survived, and even triumphed in this society that attempts in so many insidious ways to negate our being, we praise you for those whom you have raised among us to serve as role models of strength, beacon lights of hope, and guideposts pointing us toward the city of freedom.

Thank you for Richard Allen and Jarena Lee, Frederick Douglass and Harriet Tubman, Denmark Vesey and Sojourner Truth, Thurgood Marshall and Daisy Bates, Rosa Parks and Fannie Lou Homer, Martin Luther King, Jr. and Malcolm X.

Thank you, Lord, for Booker T. Washington and W.E.B. Dubois. In a culture that continually promulgates and inculcates the myth of African American inferiority, thank you for giving us scholars such as W.E.B. Dubois and educators such as Booker T. Washington whose very presence exposes the falsehood of white mental superiority. Although one emphasized classes while the other stressed masses, we praise you for their differing perspectives, for diversity is one of the hallmarks of a maturing people. Thank you, God, for both African American spirituality and brain power. You have not only given us the gift of faith to pray our way through our crises, but you have also given us the mental capacity to think our way through our dilemmas.

Renew within us a quest for excellence that both Booker T. Washington and W.E.B. Dubois exemplified, and we pray that we will never bow down to the pagan altars of mediocrity.

By the grace of the One who always supplies all of our needs do we pray, amen.

Death

Death stands at the gates of the hereafter
As a sentry shrouded in fear and power,
Guarding the entrance to eternal joy and laughter
And haunting the people as they cower.

For he knows that he will meet all of them
And it won't be so grim.
He knows that all want to come within,
Though none want to see him.

There he stands, that terrible sentry,
Denying and inviting people entry;
The helpless people he haunts and taunts,
Taking from life those as he wants.

But there is a word of hope about our fate
To save us from death's cruel ways.
It is that he just stands at the gate,
But death won't last always.

For upon entry there is life
Free of grieving, sorrow, and strife
Where happiness lies in store,
Meeting loved ones who have gone before.

O God, when I first read the poem on death, I asked myself, *Isn't this a strange subject for a young man to write about? Why is my son writing about death?* Then I looked at his world and his life and I understood why.

O God, death is all around. In the midst of life, death is present. Death strikes down our young people before they really have a chance to live. Death, in the form of street violence, gang wars, drive-by shootings, and muggings over leather jackets and gold chains, takes away the flower of our youth while it is still in bud. Fatal encounters and death-dealing outbursts emerge from arguments over trifles. Death comes in slow form to those who have fallen victim to the drug scourge. Death is seen on the big screen in the theater and on the small screen in the home. Deaths are reported daily in the news.

More personally, my son has seen some of his peers buried. He has seen his grandfather buried whom he dearly loved, and he has seen me as pastor bury church members whom he has known for most of his life. So death is a subject that he would reflect on.

However, as I read his poem, I noticed his lack of fear and the hope born of faith. I praise you for the hope that is ours as believers, the hope that now lives within the heart of my son. As a parent I pray that you would keep my children as they daily walk through mean streets. O God, hold them in your hands. Keep them from hurt, harm, and danger and bless them with long life that they might glorify you and fulfill their potential. This is my daily, heartfelt prayer that I lift before you. O God, have mercy. In Jesus' name, amen.

After

After seeds no longer find their warm resting place
And eagles keen and strong fall from their lofty grace,
Crashing to the earth, no ear to hear their groans,
No scavengers remain to rip the flesh from their bones.

When there are no more blades of grass to hold the drops of dew
That turn into splendid prisms as the sunlight passes through;
No wind to tease the broken leaves of dusky subtle hues
That rest upon the silky skin of the lake no longer blue.

When mountains lose their shape, falling to earth like snow,
Soft and smooth, sealing the surface of the jagged rocks below;
As the molten rock of the earth cools and volcanoes cease to glow,
Leaving hard, blackened rock from which nothing will ever grow.

When the earth breaks into tiny pieces, like caking, rusted tin,
And space swallows the fragments, holding them deep within
Its lifeless voids of nothingness; then if only I remain,
Then I will stand alone to hold up my blessed Jesus' name.

O Incarnate and Triune God, you abide forever. You know, Lord, how often we humans spend our lives pursuing things that really don't matter in the long run—things that moths corrupt, thieves steal, and time corrodes; things that won't give comfort in a lonely hour or bring peace to a troubled soul or satisfy the deep cravings of the human spirit.

For our preoccupation with the mundane and for our fascination with the unholy, we pray for your forgiveness.

In the midst of mind-boggling, faith-shaking, and foundation- removing changes, we are grateful for you who abides forever, whose word is sure and whose promises are secure. The gift of personal faith is this, that the God of the eternal ages is also the God who answers individual prayer. Thank you for being our God, individually and personally. Thank you for Jesus, who died not only for the whole world, but for each of us individually and personally. He intercedes for each of us—individually and personally. According to his promise, one day he's coming back again for each of us—individually and personally. For this complete, eternal story of the Good News, I thank you.

Now, Lord, I praise you that Matthew knows you for himself. It is a marvelous experience, Lord, to see the faith that I first saw in my great-grandmother, then in my grandmother, then in my mother and father, and that now dwells in Muriel and me, now dwelling in our seed and in those who are flesh of our flesh and bone of our bone. As he continues to grow and as you walk with him through some of the narrow and difficult places further up the road, I pray that his love for you will grow even deeper and his devotion for you will match the beauty of his poetic word. Amen.

The Legacy Continues—
A Son's Prayer

Father God up in heaven,
You who causes the sea to roll
But at the same time keeps it even
So it won't cross the earth's fold.

It is once again I come
To pray on bended knee
In the wonderful name of your son,
Jesus, the man from Galilee.

Thank you for the crown they placed upon his head;
Thank you for the cross he bore in my stead;
Thank you for the side from which my Savior bled,
And for moving the stone and raising him from the dead.

Thank you for your spiritual bread of yesterday.
I pray, Gracious Provider, for another portion today
That I may be uplifted, strengthened, and renewed
To fight any opposing spirit that may intrude.

Maker of the sun and architect of the celestial plan,
Inventor of the planets and creator of man,
Thou in whom I trust and whom I fear,
Forgive my transgressions and draw me ever near.

Direct, protect, and resurrect this body of clay;
Inspect, forget, and correct any wrong I may do or say;
Anoint me with your cherished, loving nectar
That I may sing praises to you, my protector.

Then one day I will see my Savior's face
As he sits with his Father in majesty and grace.
Realizing my struggle is over and victory is won,
I'll hear him say, "My good and faithful servant, well done!"